# Personal protective equipment at work (Second edition)

Personal Protective Equipment at Work
Regulations 1992 (as amended)

Guidance on Regulations

HSE Books

© *Crown copyright 2005*

*First published 1992*
*Second edition 2005*

ISBN 0 7176 6139 3

# Contents

# Introduction

1    The Personal Protective Equipment at Work Regulations came into force on 1 January 1993. They have subsequently been amended by the Police (Health and Safety) Regulations 1999 (SI 1999/860), the Health and Safety (Miscellaneous Amendments) Regulations 2002 (SI 2002/2174) and the Ionising Radiations Regulations 1999 (SI 1999/3232). This revised publication sets out changes to regulations 3, 4, 6 and 9 and provides new guidance on these changes. It also reflects the latest developments in most personal protective equipment (PPE). Part 1 sets out the Regulations, followed by guidance on each regulation. Part 2 includes more details on the types of PPE available, hazards that may require PPE to be used and advice on selection, use and maintenance.

2    The Regulations are made under the Health and Safety at Work etc Act 1974 (HSW Act) and apply to all workplaces in Great Britain.

3    The Regulations are based on European Community (EC) Directive 89/656/EEC requiring similar basic laws throughout the Community on the use of PPE in the workplace.

4    The revised guidance on the Regulations has been prepared by the Health and Safety Executive (HSE) on behalf of the Health and Safety Commission (HSC) after consultation with industry. It sets out the main steps required to comply with the Regulations.

## Consulting employees and safety representatives

5    When implementing health and safety measures, which includes the selection and use of PPE, you must consult:

(a)    safety representatives appointed by recognised trade unions; and

(b)    where there are employees who are not represented by such representatives, those employees, either directly, or indirectly through elected representatives.

6    See the free HSE leaflet INDG232 *Consulting employees on health and safety: A guide to the law*.[1]

7    Consultation with those who do the work and wear PPE is crucial to make sure the correct PPE is chosen and that it is used and maintained properly. Proper consultation can make a significant contribution to creating and maintaining a safe and healthy working environment and an effective health and safety culture. This can also benefit business by reducing the number of accidents and cases of work-related ill health.

## PART 1

# GUIDANCE ON THE PERSONAL PROTECTIVE EQUIPMENT AT WORK REGULATIONS 1992

## Regulation 1

| |
|---|
| Regulation 1 |

### Citation and commencement

*These Regulations may be cited as the Personal Protective Equipment at Work Regulations 1992 and shall come into force on 1st January 1993.*

## Regulation 2

| |
|---|
| Regulation<br><br><br><br><br><br><br><br><br><br>2 |

### Interpretation

*(1)   In these Regulations, unless the context otherwise requires, "personal protective equipment" means all equipment (including clothing affording protection against the weather) which is intended to be worn or held by a person at work and which protects him against one or more risks to his health or safety, and any addition or accessory designed to meet that objective.*

*(2)   Any reference in these Regulations to –*

*(a)   a numbered regulation or Schedule is a reference to the regulation or Schedule in these Regulations so numbered; and*

*(b)   a numbered paragraph is a reference to the paragraph so numbered in the regulation in which the reference appears.*

## Regulation 3

| |
|---|
| Regulation<br><br><br><br><br><br><br><br><br><br><br><br><br><br><br><br><br><br><br><br>3 |

### Disapplication of these Regulations

*(1)   These Regulations shall not apply to or in relation to the master or crew of a sea-going ship or to the employer of such persons in respect of the normal ship-board activities of a ship's crew under the direction of the master.*

*(2)   Regulations 4 to 12 shall not apply in respect of personal protective equipment which is –*

*(a)   ordinary working clothes and uniforms which do not specifically protect the health and safety of the wearer;*

*(b)   an offensive weapon within the meaning of section 1(4) of the Prevention of Crime Act 1953 used as self-defence or as deterrent equipment;*

*(c)   portable devices for detecting and signalling risks and nuisances;*

*(d)   personal protective equipment used for protection while travelling on a road within the meaning (in England and Wales) of section 192(1) of the Road Traffic Act 1988, and (in Scotland) of section 151 of the Roads (Scotland) Act 1984;*

*(e)   equipment used during the playing of competitive sports.*

*(3)   Regulations 4 and 6 to 12 shall not apply where any of the following Regulations apply and in respect of any risk to a person's health or safety for which any of them require the provision or use of personal protective equipment, namely –*

(a)   the Control of Lead at Work Regulations 1980;[a]

(b)   [the Ionising Radiations Regulations 1999 [SI 1999/3232];[b]

(c)   the Control of Asbestos at Work Regulations 1987;[c]

(d)   the Control of Substances Hazardous to Health Regulations 1988;[d]

(e)   the Noise at Work Regulations 1989;

(f)   the Construction (Head Protection) Regulations 1989.

(a) Now replaced by the Control of Lead at Work Regulations 2002.
(b) Paragraph 3(b) words in square brackets substituted by SI 1999/3232 regulation 41(1), Schedule 9, paragraph 3.
(c) Now replaced by the Control of Asbestos at Work Regulations 2002.
(d) Now replaced by the Control of Substances Hazardous to Health Regulations 2002 (as amended).

3

## Clothing

8     The Regulations do not apply to the following types of clothing:

(a)   uniforms provided for the primary purpose of presenting a corporate image;

(b)   ordinary working clothes; and

(c)   'protective clothing' provided in the food industry primarily for food hygiene purposes.

9     However, where any uniform or clothing protects against a specific risk to health and safety, for example high-visibility clothing worn by the emergency services, it will be subject to the Regulations. Weatherproof or insulated clothing is subject to the Regulations if it is worn to protect employees against risks to their health or safety, but not otherwise.

## Helmets

10    The Regulations do not cover the use of PPE such as cycle helmets or crash helmets worn by employees on the roads. Motorcycle crash helmets are legally required for motorcyclists under road traffic legislation. The Regulations do apply to the use of such equipment at work elsewhere if there is a risk to health and safety, for example, farm workers riding motorcycles or 'all-terrain' vehicles should use crash helmets.

## Professional sports people

11    The Regulations do not require professional sports people to use PPE such as shin guards or head protection during competition. However, they do apply to sports equipment used in other work circumstances, for example, life jackets worn by professional canoeing instructors, riding helmets worn by stable staff, or climbing helmets worn by steeplejacks.

3

## Risk of physical violence

12   The Regulations apply to the provision of PPE (such as helmets or body armour) where staff are at risk from physical violence. Where a risk assessment considers personal sirens or alarms should be provided they would be covered by the Provision and Use of Work Equipment Regulations 1998.

## Radiation dosemeters

13   The Regulations do not cover personal gas detectors or radiation dosemeters. Although this equipment would come within the broad definition of PPE, it is excluded as many of the Regulations would not be appropriate to it (for example, the fitting and ergonomic requirements of regulation 4). However, employers will have a duty to provide such equipment under section 2 of the HSW Act if its use is necessary to ensure the health and safety of employees.

## Application to merchant shipping

14   Sea-going ships are subject to separate merchant shipping legislation, administered by the Department of Transport, which gives protection to people on board. Regulation 3(1) disapplies the Regulations in respect of the normal ship-board activities of a ship's crew under the direction of the master. But it does not disapply them in respect of other work activities, for example, where a shore-based contractor goes on-board ship to carry out work on that ship. That person's activities will be subject to the Regulations within territorial waters as provided for by regulation 13. Regulation 3(1) refers to the crew of sea-going ships only. The Regulations will apply to PPE used on ships that only operate on inland waters.

## Application to aircraft

15   Aircraft are subject to these Regulations while on the ground and in airspace over Great Britain.

## Application of other regulations

16   The sets of regulations listed in regulation 3(3) require the provision and use of certain PPE against particular hazards, and the PPE at Work Regulations will not apply where these regulations remain in force. The Regulations do not apply to hearing protectors and most respiratory protective equipment (RPE). For example, a person working with asbestos would, where necessary, have to use RPE and protective clothing under the Control of Asbestos at Work Regulations 2002, rather than the PPE at Work Regulations. However, even if the PPE at Work Regulations do not apply, the advice given in this guidance may still be useful, as the general principles of selecting and maintaining suitable PPE and training employees in its use are common to all regulations which refer to PPE.

17   There are specific PPE requirements set out in regulations relating to offshore installations, mines and docks. Employers (and others with duties under the Regulations) will have to comply with both these specific regulations and the PPE at Work Regulations.

## Application to non-employees

18   These Regulations do not apply to people who are not employees, for example voluntary workers, children while in school, students at university and visitors to worksites. However, section 3 of the HSW Act, which requires that 'It

shall be the duty of every employer to conduct his undertaking in such a way as to ensure, so far as is reasonably practicable, that persons not in his employment who may be affected thereby are not exposed to risks to their health and safety', will still apply. If an employer needs to provide PPE to comply with this duty, then, by following the requirements of these Regulations he/she will fully satisfy this duty. These Regulations do apply to trainees and students on work experience programmes.

## Regulation 4

# Provision of personal protective equipment

*(1) [Subject to paragraph (1A)][a] Every employer shall ensure that suitable personal protective equipment is provided to his employees who may be exposed to a risk to their health or safety while at work except where and to the extent that such risk has been adequately controlled by other means which are equally or more effective.*

*(1A) Where the characteristics of any policing activity are such that compliance by the relevant officer with the requirement in paragraph (1) would lead to an inevitable conflict with the exercise of police powers or performance of police duties, that requirement shall be complied with so far as is reasonably practicable.[b]*

*(2) Every self-employed person shall ensure that he is provided with suitable personal protective equipment where he may be exposed to a risk to his health or safety while at work except where and to the extent that such risk has been adequately controlled by other means which are equally or more effective.*

*(3) Without prejudice to the generality of paragraphs (1) and (2), personal protective equipment shall not be suitable unless –*

*(a) it is appropriate for the risk or risks involved, the conditions at the place where exposure to the risk may occur, and the period for which it is worn;[c]*

*(b) it takes account of ergonomic requirements and the state of health of the person or persons who may wear it, and of the characteristics of the workstation of each such person;[d]*

*(c) it is capable of fitting the wearer correctly, if necessary, after adjustments within the range for which it is designed;*

*(d) so far as is practicable, it is effective to prevent or adequately control the risk or risks involved without increasing overall risk;*

*(e) it complies with any enactment (whether in an Act or instrument) which implements in Great Britain any provision on design or manufacture with respect to health or safety in any relevant Community directive listed in Schedule 1 which is applicable to that item of personal protective equipment.*

*(a) Paragraph (1): words 'Subject to paragraph (1A),' in square brackets inserted by SI 1999/860, regulation 4(1)(2).*
*(b) Paragraph (1A): inserted by SI 1999/860, regulation 4(1)(3).*
*(c) Paragraph 3: sub-paragraph (a) substituted by SI 2002/2174 regulation 5(a).*
*(d) Paragraph 3: sub-paragraph (b) substituted by SI 2002/2174 regulation 5(a).*

*(4)   Where it is necessary to ensure that personal protective equipment is hygienic and otherwise free of risk to health, every employer and every self-employed person shall ensure that personal protective equipment provided under this regulation is provided to a person for use only by him.*[a]

*(a) Paragraph (4): inserted by SI 2002/2174, regulation 5(b).*

## Providing personal protective equipment

19   Under these Regulations, PPE should be regarded as the last resort to protect against risks to health and safety. Engineering controls and safe systems of work should be considered first. HSE's publication INDG163(rev1) *Five steps to risk assessment*[2] sets out the principles for controlling risks. In taking action ask yourself:

(a)   Can I get rid of the hazard altogether?

(b)   If not, how can I control the risks so that harm is unlikely?

20   In controlling risks the following principles should be applied, if possible in the following order:

(a)   Try a less risky option, eg use lower-voltage tools.

(b)   Prevent access to the hazard, eg by guarding.

(c)   Organise work to reduce exposure to the hazard, eg if there is a risk of falling objects, ensure restricted entry to that area if possible.

(d)   If after all the above there is still a residual risk, you will need to provide PPE, eg in areas where fumes are present.

21   There are a number of reasons for making PPE the last resort. Firstly PPE protects only the person wearing it, whereas measures controlling the risk at source can protect everyone at the workplace. Secondly, maximum levels of protection are seldom achieved with PPE in practice and the actual level of protection is difficult to assess. Effective protection is only achieved by suitable PPE, correctly fitted and maintained and properly used. Finally, PPE may restrict the wearer to some extent by limiting movement or visibility.

22   PPE is not necessary where the likelihood of a worker being made ill or injured by a work-based hazard is so low as to be insignificant. For example, in most workplaces there will be some risk of people dropping objects onto their feet, but it is only when there is manual handling of objects which are heavy enough to injure the feet that the risk will be high enough to require the provision of safety footwear.

23   When providing PPE for their employees, employers need to ensure that equipment is readily available, and employees have clear instructions on where they can obtain it. Most PPE is provided on a personal basis, but may be shared by employees, for example where it is only required for limited periods. When shared, employers need to ensure such equipment is properly cleaned and, where required, decontaminated to ensure there are no health risks to the next person using it.

24   The Police (Health and Safety) Regulations 1999 extended the Regulations to the police force. They will have to provide suitable PPE (unless there are strong good operational reasons not to) and comply with the provisions set out in these Regulations.

25   The PPE used should adequately control risks. However, no PPE will provide complete protection against the risk (for example firefighters' protective clothing can give only limited protection from radiant heat and flames).

26   The use of PPE must not increase the overall level of risk, ie PPE must not be worn if the risk caused by wearing it is greater than the risk against which it is meant to protect.

## Mobile/agency workers

27   In some industries, particularly those where mobile and agency workers are engaged under a contract of employment (such as contract maintenance workers or building workers) the site operator may be better placed to provide the appropriate PPE than the mobile worker's employer or the agency. Although under these circumstances the mobile worker's employer or agency does not have to repeat the provision of suitable PPE, it is still their responsibility to ensure that suitable PPE is provided. Similarly, the site operator may in practice take the action necessary to meet the requirements of the Regulations, but the mobile worker's employer or agency still remains responsible for ensuring that this has been done.

## Charging for providing PPE

28   Under section 9 of the HSW Act, no charge can be made to the worker for the provision of PPE which is used only at work. Section 9 of the HSW Act states: 'No employer shall levy or permit to be levied on any employee of his any charge in respect of anything done or provided in pursuance of any specific requirement of the relevant statutory provisions'. Section 9 applies to these Regulations because they impose a 'specific requirement', ie to provide PPE. It also relates to all charges including returnable deposits. An employer cannot ask for money to be paid to them by an employee for the provision of PPE whether returnable or otherwise.

29   If employment has been terminated and the employee keeps the PPE without the employer's permission, then provided it has been stipulated in the contract of employment, the employer may be able to deduct the cost of replacement from any wages owed.

30   You cannot charge agency workers who are your employees (or who may be legally regarded as your employees) for PPE, or ask them to pay a refundable deposit on PPE you are lending them. You can charge a worker for PPE if they are genuinely self-employed. If you are a hirer providing PPE to a worker employed by an employment business you can make a charging arrangement with the employment business, but the employment business cannot pass the charge on to the worker or permit you to charge the worker directly.

## Suitability of PPE

31   Regulation 4(3)(a) to (e) lists factors which determine whether PPE is suitable. When selecting PPE you should consider and take account of the following factors:

(a)   The job itself and the risks for which protection is needed. For example, if there is a risk from falling objects, consider providing suitable industrial safety helmets. Other factors to consider are, for example, the physical effort needed to do the job, how long the PPE needs to be worn, and the requirements for visibility and communication.

(b)   The environment. Consider the surrounding conditions, for example the weather if working outside, heating, noise, atmospheric conditions etc.

(c)   The person. Consider the health of the person wearing the PPE and its ergonomic effects. PPE made of certain materials should not be issued to workers if they are known to cause allergies, for example latex gloves. Heavy or bulky suits can cause or make worse existing musculoskeletal problems and cause thermal comfort problems. The aim should be to choose PPE which will give maximum protection while ensuring minimum discomfort to the wearer, as uncomfortable equipment is unlikely to be worn properly.

32   Those who do the job are usually best placed to know what is involved, and they should be consulted and involved in the selection and specification of the equipment – there is a better chance of PPE being used effectively if it is accepted by each wearer.

33   There will be considerable differences in the physical dimensions of different workers and therefore more than one type or size of PPE may be needed. The required range may not be available from a single supplier.

## Personal Protective Equipment Regulations 2002 and CE marking

34   Employers should ensure that any PPE they buy bears a 'CE' mark and complies with the Personal Protective Equipment Regulations 2002 (SI 2002/1144) concerning the design or manufacture of PPE with regard to health and safety. These Regulations, which revoked the Personal Protective Equipment (EC Directive) Regulations 1992 and its amendments, implement the Personal Protective Equipment (PPE) Directive 89/686/EEC which requires manufacturers to CE mark their products (whether intended for people at work or the wider public) to show compliance with the Directive. Further information is available on the DTI website (http://www.dti.gov.uk/strd/cemark.html).

35   Products may be given a CE marking under a number of Directives and PPE could have been certified under another Directive and CE marked accordingly. If you use PPE for providing protection against health and safety hazards, you should seek confirmation from the supplier that the PPE certified satisfies the requirements of the PPE Directive.

36   PPE designed and manufactured specifically for use by the armed forces or in the maintenance of law and order (helmets, shields etc) and PPE intended for the protection or rescue of people on vessels or aircraft, which is not worn all the time, do not need to be CE marked.

37   PPE which was placed on the market before 1 July 1995 and is still suitable for the use to which it is being put and is properly maintained does not need to be CE marked.

38   The use of suitable PPE should cause no problem to healthy adults. Where problems occur, employers should seek medical advice as to whether the individual can tolerate wearing the PPE. The requirement for CE marking may be relaxed to meet the needs of the disabled and allow PPE to be customised so that it can

4

better protect them. However, there is no exception from the Regulations for disabled people, but PPE must be provided and worn if the risk assessment indicates that is what is required. For example, someone with one leg shorter than the other may require the manufacturer to adapt the safety shoe with a raised sole and this would be counted as manufacturing a new article of PPE. In this case, under a proposed amendment to the EC Directive, the custom-made article would not need the specific conformity assessment procedure that would normally be required for a CE mark. While the proposed amendment has still to be negotiated and transposed into UK law, enforcing authorities will not take any action against organisations who adapt PPE for legitimate reasons. The individual or company that customises an article of PPE needs to draw up a statement that contains the following:

(a) Data allowing identification of the specific articles of PPE.

(b) A statement that the PPE is intended for exclusive use by a particular intended user, together with the name of the intended user.

(c) The name and address of the manufacturer.

(d) The particular features of the PPE.

(e) A statement that the PPE in question conforms to the principles laid down in Annex II of the PPE Directive.

(f) A statement of the medical or technical grounds for the custom-made PPE together with the scope and number of PPE items concerned.

39 The statement must be kept for at least ten years after the PPE is placed on the market.

## Regulation 5

# Compatibility of personal protective equipment

*(1) Every employer shall ensure that where the presence of more than one risk to health or safety makes it necessary for his employee to wear or use simultaneously more than one item of personal protective equipment, such equipment is compatible and continues to be effective against the risk or risks in question.*

*(2) Every self-employed person shall ensure that where the presence of more than one risk to health or safety makes it necessary for him to wear or use simultaneously more than one item of personal protective equipment, such equipment is compatible and continues to be effective against the risk or risks in question.*

40 If more than one item of PPE is being worn, the different items of PPE must be compatible with each other. In such cases, when selecting PPE it should be ensured that all items, when used together, would adequately control the risks against which they are provided to protect. For example, certain types of half-mask respirator and goggles worn together can prevent one or both items fitting correctly, leading to increased risk of eye injury and/or respiratory exposure.

## Regulation 6     Assessment of personal protective equipment

*(1)   Before choosing any personal protective equipment which by virtue of regulation 4 he is required to ensure is provided, an employer or self-employed person shall ensure that an assessment is made to determine whether the personal protective equipment he intends to provide will be suitable.*

*(2)   The assessment required by paragraph (1) shall include –*

*(a)   an assessment of any risk or risks to health or safety which have not been avoided by other means;*

*(b)   the definition of the characteristics which personal protective equipment must have in order to be effective against the risks referred to in sub-paragraph (a) of this paragraph, taking into account any risks which the equipment itself may create;*

*(c)   comparison of the characteristics of the personal protective equipment available with the characteristics referred to in sub-paragraph (b) of this paragraph;*

*(d)   an assessment as to whether the personal protective equipment is compatible with other personal protective equipment which is in use and which an employee would be required to wear simultaneously.[a]*

*(3)   Every employer or self-employed person who is required by paragraph (1) to ensure that any assessment is made shall ensure that any such assessment is reviewed if –*

*(a)   there is reason to suspect that it is no longer valid; or*

*(b)   there has been a significant change in the matters to which it relates,*

*and where as a result of any such review changes in the assessment are required, the relevant employer or self-employed person shall ensure that they are made.*

6

*(a) Paragraph (2): sub-paragraph (d) inserted by SI 2002/2174, regulation 5(c).*

41   The purpose of the assessment required under regulation 6 is to ensure that the employer who needs to provide PPE chooses PPE which is correct for the particular risks involved and for the circumstances of its use. Paragraph 31 sets out the factors which need to be considered when choosing PPE.

42   In the simplest and most obvious cases, which can easily be repeated and explained at any time, the assessment to identify suitable PPE need not be recorded. In more complex cases, however, the assessment will need to be recorded and kept readily accessible.

### Selection of suitable PPE

43   Once potential hazards are known, there may be several types of PPE that would be suitable. For example, when assessing the need for eye protection, employers should first identify the types of hazard present, such as liquid splashes and projectiles, and then assess the degree of risk, for example the likely size and velocity of the projectiles. They can then select a suitable type of PPE from the

6

range of CE marked equipment available. In this case, eye protection designed for chemical splash protection and for different levels of impact resistance should be selected.

44 Once a type of CE marked PPE has been selected for a given application, further advice and information may be necessary to ensure that the equipment can provide the required protection to all those who need to wear it in the given working conditions. Manufacturers and suppliers have duties under the Personal Protective Equipment Regulations 2002 and under section 6 of the HSW Act to provide information which will help the employer in this duty. This information is usually in the form of a performance specification based on the essential health and safety requirements of the European PPE Directive. This is usually demonstrated by conforming to European (EN) or International (ISO) standards. Key PPE design requirements include:

(a) tests of PPE performance;

(b) how the PPE should be labelled; and

(c) what instructions should be supplied with the PPE.

45 At the end of this process, a range of potentially adequate and suitable PPE should be identified. Involving the end-users with regard to fit, comfort and wearability is likely to lead to better levels of user acceptance and therefore better protection.

46 Selection should be seen as only the first stage in a continuing programme which is also concerned with the proper use and maintenance of the equipment, and the training and supervision of employees.

6

## Regulation 7

# Maintenance and replacement of personal protective equipment

*(1)   Every employer shall ensure that any personal protective equipment provided to his employees is maintained (including replaced or cleaned as appropriate) in an efficient state, in efficient working order and in good repair.*

*(2)   Every self-employed person shall ensure that any personal protective equipment provided to him is maintained (including replaced or cleaned as appropriate) in an efficient state, in efficient working order and in good repair.*

7

47 An effective maintenance system includes the following:

(a) examination – checking for faults, damage, wear and tear, dirt etc;

(b) testing – to ensure PPE is operating as intended;

(c) cleaning – including disinfection if appropriate;

(d) repair;

(e) replacement.

48 In general, PPE should be examined to ensure it is in good working order before being issued to the user. Such examinations should be carried out by appropriately trained staff. It should not be issued if found to be defective. While

7

most PPE will be provided on a personal basis, some items may be used by a number of people. There should be arrangements for cleaning and disinfecting the PPE so there are no health risks to the next person using it.

49    The responsibility for carrying out maintenance together with the details of the procedures to be followed and their frequency should be put down in writing. Where appropriate, records of tests and examinations should also be kept. The maintenance programme will vary with the type of equipment and how it is used. For example, mechanical fall-arrestors will require a regular planned preventative maintenance programme which will include examination, testing and overhaul, and record keeping. However, abrasion-resistant gloves may only require periodic inspection by the user. Manufacturers' maintenance schedules and instructions should be followed.

50    The Regulations do not forbid employers asking employees to clean their own PPE (for example people working from home) but this should be stipulated in the person's contract of employment. The employer would need to ensure proper cleaning instructions are provided so there is no damage and the employer should arrange for spot checks to ensure PPE is suitable. As section 9 of the HSW Act states 'No employer shall levy or permit to be levied on any employee of his charge in respect of anything done or provided in pursuance of any specific requirement of the relevant statutory provisions'. This would mean that any costs of the cleaning material should be borne by the employer.

51    Simple repairs can be carried out by the trained wearer, for example replacing broken laces on safety shoes. More intricate repairs should be done by personnel with the required skills and technical knowledge. Only the correct spare parts as recommended by the manufacturer should be used. It is a good idea to keep a stock of spare parts. If the technical knowledge is not available inside the business then contract services are available from most manufacturers and suppliers of PPE as well as from specialist maintenance firms.

52    PPE will have a useable 'shelf life'. When it exceeds its shelf life or is so badly damaged that repair is not possible or too costly then it needs to be replaced. In certain circumstances it may be appropriate to provide a supply of disposable PPE (eg single-use coveralls). If disposable PPE is used it is important that users know when it should be discarded and replaced and how to dispose of it safely.

## Regulation 8

# Accommodation for personal protective equipment

*Where an employer or self-employed person is required, by virtue of regulation 4, to ensure personal protective equipment is provided, he shall also ensure that appropriate accommodation is provided for that personal protective equipment when it is not being used.*

53    Storage is needed as it prevents against:

(a)    damage from chemicals, sunlight, high humidity, heat and accidental knocks;

(b)    contamination from dirt and harmful substances;

(c)    the possibility of losing the PPE.

54    Accommodation may be simple, for example, pegs for weatherproof clothing or safety helmets. It need not be fixed, for example, safety spectacles could be kept by the user in a suitable carrying case, and PPE used by mobile workers such as

forestry workers can be stored in suitable containers in their vehicle. Where PPE becomes contaminated during use, it should be cleaned and decontaminated before storage, otherwise the accommodation may itself become contaminated and will also require suitable cleaning and decontamination. PPE which is ready for use should be clearly segregated from that which is awaiting repair or maintenance and clearly labelled as such so the correct PPE is chosen.

## Regulation 9

# Information, instruction and training

*(1)   Where an employer is required to ensure that personal protective equipment is provided to an employee, the employer shall also ensure that the employee is provided with such information, instruction and training as is adequate and appropriate to enable the employee to know –*

*(a)   the risk or risks which the personal protective equipment will avoid or limit;*

*(b)   the purpose for which and the manner in which personal protective equipment is to be used; and*

*(c)   any action to be taken by the employee to ensure that the personal protective equipment remains in an efficient state, in efficient working order and in good repair as required by regulation 7(1),*

*[and shall ensure that such information is kept available to employees;]*[a]

*(2)   Without prejudice to the generality of paragraph (1), the information and instruction provided by virtue of that paragraph shall not be adequate and appropriate unless it is comprehensible to the persons to whom it is provided.*

*(3)   Without prejudice to the generality of paragraph (1) the employer shall, where appropriate, and at suitable intervals, organise demonstrations in the wearing of personal protective equipment.*[b]

*(a) Paragraph 1 words 'and shall ensure that such information is kept available to employees' in square brackets inserted by SI 2002/2174, regulation 5(d).*
*(b) Paragraph 3 inserted by SI 2002/2174 regulation 5(e).*

55   The Regulations require employers to provide suitable information, instruction and training for their employees, to enable them to make effective use of the PPE provided to protect them against workplace hazards to their health and safety. A systematic approach to training is needed – this means that everyone who is involved in the use or maintenance of PPE should be trained appropriately.

56   Users must be trained in the proper use of PPE, how to correctly fit and wear it, and what its limitations are. Managers and supervisors must also be aware of why PPE is being used and how to use it properly. People involved in maintaining, repairing and testing the equipment and in its selection for use will also need training. Training should include elements of theory as well as practice in using the equipment, and should be carried out in accordance with any recommendations and instructions supplied by the PPE manufacturer.

57   The extent of the instruction and training will vary with the complexity and performance of the equipment. For PPE which is simple to use and maintain, such as safety helmets, some basic instructions to the users will be all that is required.

On the other hand, the safe use of anti-static footwear or laser eye protection will depend on an adequate understanding of the principles behind them. The instruction and training should include both theory and practice.

## Theoretical training

58    Theoretical training should include:

(a)    an explanation of the risks present and why PPE is needed;

(b)    the operation, performance and limitations of the equipment;

(c)    instructions on the selection, use and storage of PPE. Written operating procedures such as permits to work involving PPE should be explained;

(d)    factors which can affect the protection provided by the PPE such as other protective equipment, personal factors, working conditions, inadequate fitting, and defects, damage and wear;

(e)    recognising defects in PPE and arrangements for reporting loss or defects.

## Practical training

59    Practical training should include:

(a)    practice in putting on, wearing and removing the equipment;

(b)    practice in inspection and, where appropriate, testing of the PPE before use;

(c)    practice in how to maintain PPE, which can be done by the user, such as cleaning and the replacement of certain components;

(d)    instruction in the safe storage of equipment.

60    The extent of the training that is required will depend on the type of equipment, how frequently it is used and the needs of the people being trained. Many manufacturers of PPE run training courses for users of their equipment and these courses may be of particular benefit to small users who do not have training facilities.

61    As well as initial training, users of PPE and others involved with the equipment may need refresher training from time to time. Records of training details should be kept to help with the efficient administration of the training programme.

62    Employers must ensure, not only that their employees undergo the appropriate training, but also that they understand what they are being taught. Employees may have difficulty in understanding their training for a number of reasons. For example, the risks (and precautions) may be of a particularly complex nature, making it difficult for employees to understand the precise nature of the protective measures they must take. English may not be the first language of some employees who may need the training to be given in a language they understand.

## Regulation 10

### Use of personal protective equipment

*(1) Every employer shall take all reasonable steps to ensure that any personal protective equipment provided to his employees by virtue of regulation 4(1) is properly used.*

*(2) Every employee shall use any personal protective equipment provided to him by virtue of these Regulations in accordance both with any training in the use of the personal protective equipment concerned which has been received by him and the instructions respecting that use which have been provided to him by virtue of regulation 9.*

*(3) Every self-employed person shall make full and proper use of any personal protective equipment provided to him by virtue of regulation 4(2).*

*(4) Every employee and self-employed person who has been provided with personal protective equipment by virtue of regulation 4 shall take all reasonable steps to ensure that it is returned to the accommodation provided for it after use.*

63   PPE should be used in accordance with the employer's instructions, which should in turn be based on the manufacturer's instructions for use. It should be used only after adequate training and instructions have been given to the user so they understand why, how, where and when it is to be used.

64   Supervision is also vital to ensure PPE is properly used both on and off site. It is important that those with a supervisory role are also provided with adequate training and instructions so that they have the necessary skills to carry out the job. Spot checks are a useful way of monitoring how well PPE is used and corrective action can then be taken if spot checks reveal misuse.

65   Most PPE should be returned after use to the storage place provided under regulation 8. However, there may be circumstances where the employee may take PPE away from the workplace, for example mobile workers not immediately returning to the premises may take protective footwear, overalls etc home. Equipment used or worn intermittently, for example welding visors, need only be returned at the end of the working period, shift or assignment.

## Regulation 11

### Reporting loss or defect

*Every employee who has been provided with personal protective equipment by virtue of regulation 4(1) shall forthwith report to his employer any loss of or obvious defect in that personal protective equipment.*

66   Employers should make arrangements to ensure that their employees can report to them (or their representative) the loss of or defects in PPE. These arrangements should also ensure that defective PPE is repaired or replaced before the employee concerned re-starts work.

67   Employees must take reasonable care of PPE provided and report to their employer any loss or obvious defect as soon as possible. If employees have any concerns about the serviceability of the PPE, they should immediately consult their employer or the employer's representative.

## Regulation 12     Exemption certificates

(1) *The Secretary of State for Defence may, in the interests of national security, by a certificate in writing exempt –*

(a) *any of the home forces, any visiting force or any headquarters from those requirements of these Regulations which impose obligations on employers; or*

(b) *any member of the home forces, any member of a visiting force or any member of a headquarters from the requirements imposed by regulation 10 or 11;*

*and any exemption such as is specified in sub-paragraph (a) or (b) of this paragraph may be granted subject to conditions and to a limit of time and may be revoked by the said Secretary of State by a further certificate in writing at any time.*

(2) *In this regulation –*

(a) *"the home forces" has the same meaning as in section 12(1) of the Visiting Forces Act 1952;*

(b) *"headquarters" has the same meaning as in article 3(2) of the Visiting Forces and International Headquarters (Application of Law) Order 1965;*

(c) *"member of a headquarters" has the same meaning as in paragraph 1(1) of the Schedule to the International Headquarters and Defence Organisations Act 1964; and*

(d) *"visiting force" has the same meaning as it does for the purposes of any provision of Part I of the Visiting Forces Act 1952.*

**12**

## Regulation 13     Extension outside Great Britain

**Regulation**

*These Regulations shall apply to and in relation to the premises and activities outside Great Britain to which sections 1 to 59 and 80 to 82 of the Health and Safety at Work etc. Act 1974 apply by virtue of the Health and Safety at Work etc. Act 1974 (Application Outside Great Britain) Order 1989[a] as they apply within Great Britain.*

*(a) Now replaced by the Health and Safety at Work etc Act 1974 (Application Outside Great Britain) Order 2001.*

**13**

**Guidance**

68    The Regulations apply to certain work activities carried out in the territorial sea adjacent to Great Britain and in designated areas of the UK Continental Shelf except where disapplied by regulation 3. These activities are listed in the Health and Safety at Work etc Act (Application Outside Great Britain) Order 2001.

69    This applies to offshore installations, wells, pipelines, and activities carried out by vessels in connection with an offshore installation or a well such as construction, repair, dismantling, loading, unloading and diving. Also covered are other construction and similar activities carried out in territorial waters.

**13**

## Regulation 14

### Modifications, repeal and revocations

| Regulation |
| --- |
| 14 |

*(1)    The Act and Regulations specified in Schedule 2 shall be modified to the extent specified in the corresponding Part of that Schedule.*

*(2)    Section 65 of the Factories Act 1961 is repealed.*

*(3)    The instruments specified in column 1 of Schedule 3 are revoked to the extent specified in column 3 of that Schedule.*

| Guidance |
| --- |
| 14 |

70    The Regulations specified in Schedule 2 have been amended to ensure that they are consistent with the requirements of the PPE at Work Regulations, particularly with regard to the assessment and provision of suitable PPE, and accommodation for PPE.

# Schedule 1 — Relevant Community Directives

| Schedule | |
|---|---|
| | |
| 1 | |

**Regulation 4(3)(e)**

*1    Council Directive of 21 December 1989 on the approximation of the laws of the Member States relating to personal protective equipment (89/686/EEC), as amended by Council Directive 93/95/EEC of 29 October 1993 and Article 7 of Council Directive 93/63/EEC of 22 July 1993.*

*2    Council Directive 93/42/EEC concerning medical device (OJ No L169, 12 July 1993 pl).*

# Schedule 2 — Modifications

| Schedule | |
|---|---|
| | |
| 2 | |

**Regulation 14(1)**

## Part I

## The Factories Act 1961

*Section 30 of the Factories Act 1961, amended by Schedule 2 paragraph 1, has been repealed by the Confined Spaces Regulations 1997 (SI 1997/1713).*

## Part II

## The Coal and Other Mines (Fire and Rescue) Order 1956

*The Coal and Other Mines (Fire and Rescue) Regulations 1956 (SI 1956/1768), amended by Schedule 2 paragraphs 2-4, have been revoked by the Escape and Rescue from Mines Regulations 1995 (SI 1995/2870).*

## Part III

## The Shipbuilding and Ship-Repairing Regulations 1960

*The Shipbuilding and Ship-Repairing Regulations 1960 (SI 1960/1932), amended by Schedule 2 paragraph 5, have been revoked by the Dangerous Substances and Explosive Atmospheres Regulations 2002 (SI 2002/2776).*

## Part IV

## The Coal Mines (Respirable Dust) Regulations 1975

*6    In regulation 10(a), for "dust respirators of a type approved by the Executive for the purpose of this Regulation", substitute "suitable dust respirators".*

## Part V

## The Control of Lead at Work Regulations 1980

*The Control of Lead at Work Regulations 1980 (SI 1980/1248), amended by Schedule 2 paragraphs 7-12, have been revoked by the Control of Lead at Work Regulations 1998 (SI 1998/543).*

## Part VI

## The Ionising Radiations Regulations 1985

*The former paragraphs 13-15 referring to the Ionising Radiations Regulations 1985 have been revoked by the Ionising Radiations Regulations 1999.*

## Part VII

## The Control of Asbestos at Work Regulations 1987

*The Control of Asbestos at Work Regulations 1987 (SI 1987/2115), amended by Schedule 2 paragraphs 16-18, have been revoked by the Control of Asbestos at Work Regulations 2002 (SI 2002/2675).*

## Part VIII

## The Control of Substances Hazardous to Health Regulations 1988

*The Control of Substances Hazardous to Health Regulations 1988 (SI 1988/1657), amended by Schedule 2 paragraphs 19-21, have been revoked by the Control of Substances Hazardous to Health Regulations 1994 (SI 1994/3246).*

## Part IX

## The Noise at Work Regulations 1989

22    *Add the following new paragraph at the end of regulation 8 –*

*"(3) Any personal ear protectors provided by virtue of this regulation shall comply with any enactment (whether in an Act or instrument) which implements in Great Britain any provision on design or manufacture with respect to health or safety in any relevant Community directive listed in Schedule 1 to the Personal Protective Equipment at Work Regulations 1992 which is applicable to those ear protectors.".*

## Part X

## The Construction (Head Protection) Regulations 1989

23    *Add the following paragraphs at the end of regulation 3 –*

*"(3) Any head protection provided by virtue of this regulation shall comply with any enactment (whether in an Act or instrument) which implements any provision on design or manufacture with respect to health or safety in any relevant Community directive listed in Schedule 1 to the Personal Protective Equipment at Work Regulations 1992 which is applicable to that head protection.*

*(4)    Before choosing head protection, an employer or self-employed person shall make an assessment to determine whether it is suitable.*

(5) The assessment required by paragraph (4) of this regulation shall involve –

(a) the definition of the characteristics which head protection must have in order to be suitable;

(b) comparison of the characteristics of the protection available with the characteristics referred to in sub-paragraph (a) of this paragraph.

(6) The assessment required by paragraph (4) shall be reviewed if –

(a) there is reason to suspect that it is no longer valid; or

(b) there has been a significant change in the work to which it relates,

and where as a result of the review changes in the assessment are required, the relevant employer or self-employed person shall make them.

(7) Every employer and every self-employed person shall ensure that appropriate accommodation is available for head protection provided by virtue of these Regulations when it is not being used.".

24 For regulation 6(4), substitute the following paragraph –

"(4) Every employee or self-employed person who is required to wear suitable head protection by or under these Regulations shall –

(a) make full and proper use of it; and

(b) take all reasonable steps to return it to the accommodation provided for it after use.".

25 In regulation 9(2), omit the full stop and add "and that any provision imposed by the European Communities in respect of the encouragement of improvements in the safety and health of workers at work will be satisfied.".

# Schedule 3

## Revocations

### Regulation 14(3)

| (1) | (2) | (3) |
|---|---|---|
| *Title* | *Reference* | *Extent of Revocation* |
| Regulations dated 26th February 1906 in respect of the processes of spinning and weaving of flax and tow and the processes incidental thereto (the Flax and Tow-Spinning and Weaving Regulations 1906). | SR & O 1906/177, amended by SI 1988/1657. | In regulation 9, the words "unless waterproof skirts, and bibs of suitable material, are provided by the occupier and worn by the workers". Regulation 13. |
| Order dated 5th October 1917 (the Tin or Terne Plates Manufacture Welfare Order 1917). | SR & O 1917/1035. | Paragraph 1. |
| Order dated 15th August 1919 (the Fruit Preserving Welfare Order 1919). | SR & O 1919/1136, amended by Sl 1988/1657. | Paragraph 1. |
| Order dated 23rd April 1920 (the Laundries Welfare Order 1920). | SR & O 1920/654. | Paragraph 1. |
| Order dated 28th July 1920 (the Gut-Scraping, Tripe Dressing, etc. Welfare Order 1920). | SR & O 1920/1437. | Paragraph 1. |
| Order dated 3rd March 1921 (the Glass Bevelling Welfare Order 1921). | SR & O 1921/288. | Paragraph 1. |
| The Aerated Water Regulations 1921. | SR & O 1921/1932; amended by SI 1981/686 | The whole Regulations. |
| The Sacks (Cleaning and Repairing) Welfare Order 1927. | SR & O 1927/860. | Paragraph 1. |
| The Oil Cake Welfare Order 1929. | SR & O 1929/534. | Paragraph 1. |
| The Cement Works Welfare Order 1930. | SR & O 1930/94. | Paragraph 1. |
| The Tanning Welfare Order 1930. | SR & O 1930/312. | Paragraph 1 and the Schedule. |

| | (1) | (2) | (3) |
|---|---|---|---|
| **Schedule** | *Title* | *Reference* | *Extent of Revocation* |
| | The Magnesium (Grinding of Castings and Other Articles) Special Regulations 1946. | SR & O 1946/2107. | Regulation 12. |
| | The Clay Works (Welfare) Special Regulations 1948. | SI 1948/1547. | Regulation 5. |
| | The Iron and Steel Foundries Regulations 1953. | SI 1953/1464 amended by SI 1974/1681 and SI 1981/1332. | Regulation 8. |
| | The Shipbuilding and Ship-Repairing Regulations 1960. | SI 1960/1932; amended by SI 1974/1681. | Regulations 73 and 74. |
| | The Non-Ferrous Metals (Melting and Founding) Regulations 1962. | SI 1962/1667; amended by SI 1974/1681. | Regulation 13. |
| | The Abstract of Special Regulations (Aerated Water) Order 1963. | SI 1963/2058. | The whole Order. |
| | The Construction (Health and Welfare) Regulations 1966. | SI 1966/95; to which there are amendments not relevant to these regulations. | Regulation 15. |
| | The Foundries (Protective Footwear and Gaiters) Regulations 1971. | SI 1971/476. | The whole Regulations. |
| | The Protection of Eyes Regulations 1974. | SI 1974/1681; amended by SI 1975/303. | The whole Regulations. |
| **3** | The Aerated Water Regulations (Metrication) Regulations 1981. | SI 1981/686. | The whole Regulations. |

| PART 2 | SELECTION, USE AND MAINTENANCE OF PERSONAL PROTECTIVE EQUIPMENT |
|---|---|

## Introduction

71    Part 2 provides guidance to employers to help them comply with their duties to select suitable PPE, use and maintain it. It describes the PPE used for different parts of the body (head, eye and face, hand and arm, body (including the legs) and feet) and then covers PPE used to prevent drowning and falls from height.

72    The Regulations do not apply to hearing protection and to respiratory protective equipment for most work activities, as they are covered by other regulations (see paragraph 16), so they are only mentioned briefly at the end of Part 2. Note that these items of PPE need to be compatible with any other PPE provided. Full guidance on these including selection, use and maintenance can be found in the publications L108 *Reducing noise at work: Guidance on the Noise at Work Regulations 1989*[3] and HSG53 *Respiratory protective equipment at work: A practical guide.*[4]

73    Some common selection, use and maintenance points for PPE are:

(a)    PPE should be labelled to show what it protects against and is resistant to. Talk to manufacturers and suppliers on the protection offered by their products before buying. Another useful source of information is the British Safety Industry Federation (Tel: 01745 585600 Website: www.bsif.co.uk).

(b)    Always use PPE according to the manufacturer's instructions. The Personal Protective Equipment Regulations 2002 state that PPE on the market must be supplied with relevant information in the official language(s) of the country of destination on:

    (i)    storage, use, cleaning, maintenance, servicing and disinfecting;

    (ii)   the level of protection provided by the PPE;

    (iii)  suitable PPE accessories and appropriate spare parts;

    (iv)   limitations on use;

    (v)    the obsolescence period for the PPE or certain of its components.

(c)    Ensure items of PPE used together are compatible with each other to ensure they continue to be effective against the risks.

(d)    Train and instruct workers to put on and remove contaminated clothing without contaminating themselves.

(e)    **Do not** reuse disposable PPE.

(f)    **Do not** leave contaminated work areas without removing the contaminated clothing in appropriate changing areas.

(g)    **Do not** store PPE in direct sunlight or in hot and humid places as this can cause damage.

(h)    **Do not** use PPE if it is damaged or heavily worn. If it is unfit for use or past its usable protective life, dispose of it properly and replace it.

# Head protection

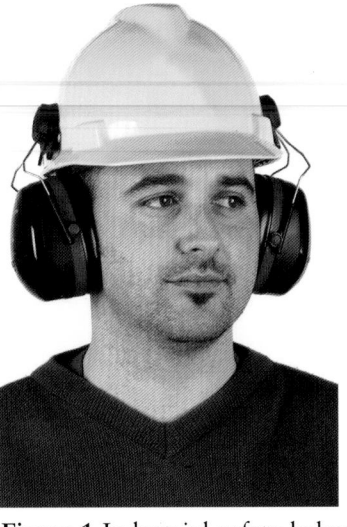

**Figure 1** Industrial safety helmet (with fitted ear defenders)

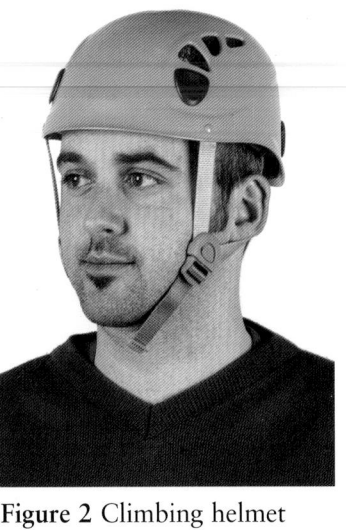

**Figure 2** Climbing helmet

## Types of protection

74    There are several types of head protection:

(a)    **Industrial safety helmets** – Protect against falling objects or impact with fixed objects and offer limited resistance to flame. Helmets are also available which give protection against impact at high or low temperatures, against electrical shock from brief contact up to 440 V ac and against molten metal splash.

(b)    **Bump caps** – Protect against bumping the head (eg walking into a fixed object) and scalping, and can stop hair getting caught in machinery and moving parts. Bump caps **do not** offer adequate protection where there is a risk of falling objects or moving or suspended loads.

(c)    **Firefighters' helmets** – These are similar to industrial safety helmets, but cover more of the head and give greater protection against impact, heat and flame.

(d)    **Transport helmets** – Protect against head injuries from falling off a motorcycle or bicycle. The PPE at Work Regulations do not cover the provision of motorcycle and bicycle helmets on the road. Motorcycle crash helmets are legally required for motorcyclists under road traffic legislation. However in off-road situations, employers should provide suitable transport helmets, for example motorcycle helmets for farm workers who use all-terrain vehicles (ATVs).

(e)    **Leisure helmets** – Helmets used for activities, such as horse riding, canoeing or climbing, which protect against the risks of that particular activity.

## Examples of hazards which may require head protection

75    Examples of hazards or situations where head protection may be required are:

(a)  low-level fixed objects, for example pipework, machines or scaffolding where there is a risk of collision;

(b)  transport activities, hoists, lifting plant, conveyors etc involving the risk of falling material;

(c)  tree-felling;

(d)  blasting work, for example in quarries, opencast mining etc;

(e)  under the Construction (Head Protection) Regulations 1989, employers must take all reasonably practicable measures to ensure that suitable head protection is worn (except by turban-wearing Sikhs) on construction sites unless there is no foreseeable risk of head injury other than by falling;

(f)  under the Docks Regulations 1988, suitable safety helmets must be worn by those working in docks premises where there is a foreseeable risk of injury to the head and employees must wear the helmets in a proper manner when working there.

## Key points

76  The key points to note for head protection are:

(a)  Use an adjustable chinstrap, if fitted, to make sure the helmet does not fall off.

(b)  Clean the inside of the helmet and clean or replace sweatbands regularly.

(c)  Check regularly that any damage to the outside is no more than shallow scratches or grazes and that the internal harness is not damaged or deformed.

(d)  Throw head protection away after significant impact by a fixed or falling object. Head protection is unfit for use if the outside is deeply scratched, worn or deformed, the harness is damaged or deformed or it is beyond its usable protective life.*

(e)  Wear the helmet so that the brim is level when the head is upright. **Do not** wear it sloping up or down as this may significantly reduce the protection it can provide.

(f)  **Do not** wear head protection back to front – it will not protect you if you do.

(g)  **Do not** customise head protection, eg make your own ventilation holes, paint, mark or put stickers on it.

(h)  **Do not** wear a baseball-style bump cap where there is a risk of falling objects – wear an industrial safety helmet instead.

* As a general guide, industrial safety helmets should be replaced three years after manufacture, but always check with the manufacturer.

# Eye and face protection

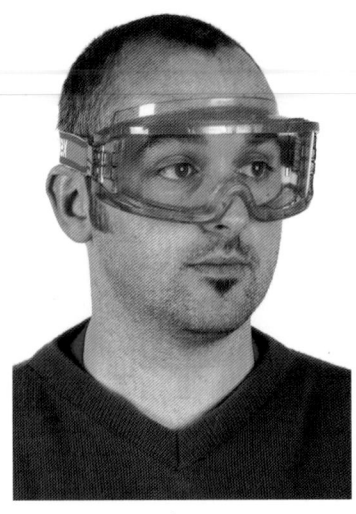 

**Figure 3** Goggles          **Figure 4** Faceshield

## Types of protection

77    The main types of eye and face protection are:

(a)    **Safety spectacles** – May be separate lenses in a metal or plastic frame (similar in appearance to prescription glasses) or have a single lens/frame moulding (sometimes called eyeshields). Most designs have side shields. Spectacles can incorporate corrective lenses, while eyeshields may fit over prescription glasses.

(b)    **Goggles** – These are made with a flexible plastic frame and one or two lenses with a flexible elastic headband. They give the eyes protection from all angles as the complete rim is in contact with the face. Some goggles are ventilated and may be unsuitable for protection against gases and fine dusts.

(c)    **Faceshields** – These have one large lens with a frame and adjustable head harness or are mounted on a helmet. Most can be worn with prescription glasses. They protect the face but do not fully enclose the eyes.

## Examples of hazards which may require eye and face protection

78    The main hazards are:

(a)    Liquid or chemical splash as a result of handling or coming into contact with dangerous liquids or chemical substances.

(b)    Working with power-driven tools, where chippings or debris are likely to fly into the face, or abrasive materials may be projected.

(c)    Dust, gas or liquid mist from machines, high-pressure cleaning, or using gas or vapour under pressure.

(d)    Radiant heat, molten metal, hot solids, sparks or hot liquid splash from working in hot conditions, for example welding, ovens, furnaces etc.

(e)    Intense light or other optical radiation emitted at levels liable to cause risk of injury, for example welding, lasers etc.

## Key points

79    The key points to note for eye and face protection are:

(a)    Make sure the eye/face protection fits the user and does not fall off easily. It should be issued on a personal basis.

(b)    Consider misting/fogging. Anti-mist and ventilated eye protection is available.

(c)    Store eye protection in a protective case.

(d)    Follow the manufacturer's instructions on cleaning, not forgetting headbands and frames. Use only anti-mist, cleaning and anti-static fluids and cloths recommended by the manufacturer.

(e)    **Do not** use when visibility is noticeably reduced (eg the lenses are deeply scratched or worn) or the frame, headband or harness is deformed. Throw them away and replace them.

# Hand and arm protection

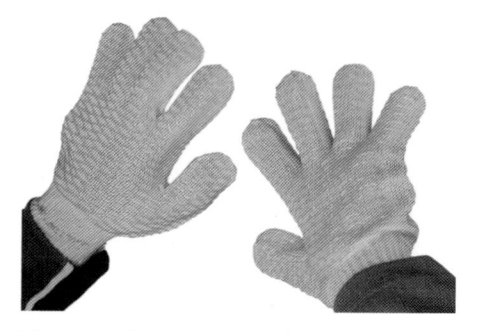

**Figure 5** Cut-resistant gloves

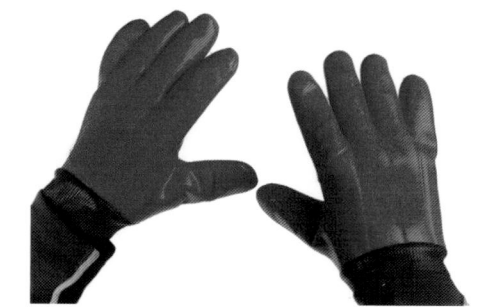

**Figure 6** Gloves for hand protection in the cold

## Types of protection

80    There are four types of hand and arm protection:

(a)    **Gloves** – hand only.

(b)    **Gloves with a cuff** – hand and wrist.

(c)    **Gauntlets/sleeves/long gloves** – hand, wrist and part of forearm.

(d)    **Sleeving/arm protection** – part or whole of forearm and/or upper arm.

## Examples of hazards which may require hand/arm protection

81    Some examples where hand and arm protection may be required are:

(a)    Protection from cuts and abrasions, for example when handling sharp or pointed objects.

(b)     To keep hands warm and supple in cold weather, for example when working on a building site, as manual dexterity is lost when the hands are cold.

(c)     To keep hands warm in cold weather when operating machines that cause vibration, such as pneumatic drills and chainsaws. Vibration white finger occurs more often and more severely when the hands and fingers are cold as the blood supply to the fingers is reduced by the body in an attempt to conserve heat.

(d)     Danger from electrical hazards – see paragraph 85(c) for further information.

(e)     Handling or coming into contact with chemicals, for example maintenance of machinery, cleaning up chemical spillages and mixing and dispensing pesticide formulations.

(f)     Handling radioactive materials.

(g)     Handling hot or cold materials and work involving accidental contact with naked flames such as welding, ovens etc.

## Key points

82      The key points to note for hand and arm protection are:

(a)     Make sure that users are not allergic to or sensitised by the material, for example latex gloves are made of rubber and the proteins present in the rubber are skin and respiratory sensitisers. If you have to use latex gloves, use a powder-free type containing a minimum amount of free proteins. It may be better to select an alternative material, if practicable.

(b)     Ensure they fit the wearer properly and are worn correctly for the job being done. For example there should be no gap between the glove and the wearer's sleeve when handling dangerous chemicals.

(c)     Ensure users can handle and remove the gloves carefully to avoid contamination of the hands and the inside of the glove. Contaminants that get inside the glove and sit permanently against the skin may cause greater exposure than if a glove had not been worn at all. Many wearers are not instructed on how to correctly put on and take off gloves, which means that the insides of the gloves become contaminated when worn for the second time or more. This contamination can cause damage to the skin.

(d)     Ensure users clean their hands thoroughly when they change gloves and moisturise their hands at least once a day.

(e)     Check gloves regularly and throw them away if they are worn or have deteriorated. They should be free of holes or cuts and debris and their shape should not be distorted.

(f)     **Do not** wear a glove for extended periods as this can lead to the development of excessive moisture (sweat) on the skin which in itself will act as an irritant.

(g)     **Do not** use pre-work creams, sometimes sold as barrier creams, as a replacement for carefully selected gloves. They are not PPE because:

        (i)     they do not provide protection against hazards;

(ii) workers may not apply them properly, leaving part of their skin uncovered;

(iii) there is no information available on the rate of penetration of substances through pre-work creams; and

(iv) protection may be removed while working without workers noticing.

(h) Select carefully for chemical resistance and protection, especially against mixtures, and do not use for longer than the recommended breakthrough times. Manufacturers will advise on breakthrough times for their products.

## Protective clothing (including the legs)

**Figure 7** Cut-resistant chain mail apron

### Types of protection

83 Protective clothing must offer some specific protection – if it does not, it is classified as 'workwear'. There are three main types of protective clothing:

(a) **Separates** – jackets, trousers etc that only cover part of the body.

(b) **Aprons** – that only cover part of the body.

(c) **Overalls, coveralls and body suits** – which cover the whole body.

84 As well as trousers for leg protection there are also knee pads and gaiters. Hard fibre or metal guards will help protect against some impacts.

### Examples of hazards which may require protective clothing

85 The main hazards are:

(a) Working with chemicals – handling small quantities of low-risk chemicals may only require aprons protecting against accidental splashes. Larger quantities of chemical or risks of contact with sprays or jets of chemical are likely to require protective coats/trousers or coveralls. Potential exposures to large quantities of chemical or very hazardous materials will often require the use of gas- or liquid-tight suits and appropriate RPE.

(b)     Cuts and hazards working with knives, machinery etc – use clothing made of thick or padded material or multi-layer reinforced fabric, aramid fibres (eg body armour material) or chain mail.*, †

(c)     Electrical hazards – use electrical insulating clothing when working on or near live parts of low-voltage installations at nominal voltages up to 500 V ac or 750 V dc. The clothing needs to be used with other electrical insulating PPE, such as boots and gloves. It prevents electrocution when there is a risk of unintentional contact with live parts. Use conductive clothing for live working (especially bare-hand working) at a nominal voltage up to 800 kV ac. This clothing also includes gloves, shoes, mitts and hoods.

(d)     Electrostatic hazards – where clothing is to be used in potentially explosive atmospheres, select clothing made from materials which have been shown to resist the build-up of static electricity.

(e)     Cold from working outside or in a cold/freezer area – use clothing made of thick or padded material or multi-layer leather or fabric or thermal insulating fabrics. Minus 25 and Minus 50 suits are available which are designed to protect at these sub-zero temperatures.

(f)     Wet when working outside in the rain or using water sprays for cleaning etc – use rubbers, plastics, water-repellent coatings, waterproof and breathable fabrics.

(g)     Radiant heat and flame from welding, metalworking, foundries – use suitable flame-retardant, insulating and heat-resistant fabrics.

## Key points

86     The key points to note about protective clothing are:

(a)     Store used/contaminated clothing separately from clean clothing.

(b)     Select protective clothing carefully for chemical resistance and protection, especially against mixtures, and do not use for longer than the recommended breakthrough times. Manufacturers will advise on breakthrough times for their products.

(c)     Clean clothing according to the manufacturer's instructions. For chemical suits hygienic cleaning may be possible but industry guidance is that this clothing cannot be effectively decontaminated.

(d)     Inspect for wear and tear, loose seams and surface damage before use.

(e)     **Do not** wear loose protective clothing near moving machinery in case it gets caught.

* Butchers and slaughterhouse workers should wear plate-link or chain mail aprons if there is a risk of injury to the abdomen or chest, for example using knives or choppers.

† Chainsaw protective clothing – The front of the leg is the most vulnerable to chainsaw accidents although the back of the leg is at risk. Protective legwear incorporates layers of loosely woven long synthetic fibres. On contact with the chainsaw, the fibres are drawn out and clog the chainsaw sprocket, causing the chain to stop. Legwear is available with all-round protection or with protection only for the front of the legs. The legwear with all-round protection offers the greatest protection for users. Jackets and gloves are also available with inserts of chainsaw-resistant materials at vulnerable points.

# High-visibility clothing

**Figure 8** High-visibility waterproof jacket

87    Most high-visibility clothing has a fluorescent yellow or orange background, made from materials impregnated with fluorescent pigments, with bands of shiny retroflective material. It is designed to make the wearer easy to see under any light conditions in the day and under illumination, for example by vehicle headlights in the dark.

## Types of high-visibility clothing

88    There are three classes of high-visibility clothing. Each has minimum areas for the background and retroflective bands:

(a)    **Class 1** – the least conspicuous (waistcoats and most trousers).

(b)    **Class 2** – more conspicuous than Class 1 (waistcoats, jackets and some trousers).

(c)    **Class 3** – the most conspicuous (jackets and coveralls).

## Examples of use

89    High-visibility clothing is used as follows:

(a)    Some industries specify a background colour, eg fluorescent orange is used as the background colour for railway work as specified in Railway Group Standard GO/RT3279.

(b)    Some industries may specify the type of clothing, eg the Code of Practice to the New Roads and Street Works Act 1991 as modified in 2002 requires Class 2 or 3 waistcoats or jackets for road work. Class 3 jackets (ie full-length sleeves) should be worn on dual-carriageway roads with a speed limit of 50 mph or above.

(c)    The Docks Regulations 1988 require those on foot to wear high-visibility clothing in docks premises:

(i)    where roll-on and roll-off operations are carried out;

(ii)  where work with straddle carriers is carried out; and

(iii)  where there is a lorry park and there is a danger of being hit by vehicles.

(d)  Working in construction sites.

(e)  Airport workers loading and unloading aeroplanes.

## Key points

90  The key points to note for high-visibility clothing are:

(a)  Select high-visibility clothing suitable for the task. Clothing that protects from other hazards such as cold weather is often available with a high-visibility option. Outdoor workers may need different clothing at different times of the year.

(b)  Inspect before use for wear and tear, or loose seams.

(c)  Ensure only correct cleaning materials are used. Lack of cleanliness is a significant factor in loss of visibility.

# Foot protection

**Figure 9** Foundry boots

**Figure 10** Thermally lined boots for cold work

## Types of protection

91  Footwear is available in a range of styles, for example shoe, low ankle boot, high ankle boot, knee boot, thigh boot and even chest-high waders. The different types of protective footwear include the following:

(a)  **Safety boots or shoes** – These are the most common type of safety footwear. They normally have protective toe-caps and may also have other safety features including slip-resistant soles, penetration-resistant mid-soles and insulation against extremes of heat and cold.

(b)  **Wellington boots** – These are usually made of rubber and used for working in wet conditions. They are also useful in jobs where the footwear needs to be washed and disinfected for hygiene reasons, eg in the food industry and the chemical industry.

(c)  **Clogs** – These may also be used as safety footwear. They are traditionally made from beech wood and may be fitted with steel toe-caps and thin rubber soles for quieter tread.

(d) **Footwear for specific tasks** – These protect against hazards in these areas, for example foundry boots and chainsaw boots.

## Examples of hazards which may require foot protection

92    The main hazards which may need foot protection are:

(a) Objects falling on and crushing the foot/toes – this will include jobs requiring manual handling, such as construction workers or removal people.

(b) Treading on pointed or sharp objects (eg nails) on the ground piercing the shoe, injuring the sole of the foot and resulting in cuts and wounds.

(c) Slips, trips and falls resulting in injuries such as sprained ankles. Although there is no such thing as non-slip footwear there are slip-resistant 'anti-slip' soles which can reduce the likelihood of slipping on certain floors.

(d) Working in cold or hot conditions. Working in the cold requires footwear with thermal insulation. Work in hot conditions requires footwear with heat-resistant and insulating soles. For protection against molten metal splash, footwear must have quick-release fastenings.

(e) Electrical hazards (see paragraph 85(c) for further information).

(f) Working in potentially explosive atmospheres or for the handling of sensitive materials (eg detonators). Footwear must be anti-static.

(g) Working with and handling hazardous chemicals. Footwear should be impermeable and resistant to that chemical.

(h) Wet work, for example using water sprays when cleaning. Water-resistant or waterproof material should be used. Wellington boot style footwear should be used for very wet work.

## Key points

93    Key points to note about protective footwear are:

(a) Consider the comfort factors for the wearer. Generally footwear should be flexible, wet-resistant and absorb perspiration. Cushioned soles make standing more comfortable.

(b) Inspect for wear and tear and loose seams before use. Replace broken laces and remove materials lodged in the tread of the sole.

## Drowning protection – buoyancy aids, life jackets and immersion suits

94    Life jackets or buoyancy aids should be worn where there is a foreseeable risk of drowning when working near water. Buoyancy aids are worn to provide extra buoyancy to help a conscious person keep afloat. However, they will not turn over an unconscious person from a face-down position. Life jackets provide enough buoyancy to turn even an unconscious person face upwards within five seconds (ten seconds if automatically inflated). The person's head should be supported with the mouth and nose clear of the water.

## Types of life jackets/buoyancy aids

95    There are four types of life jackets/buoyancy aids:

(a)    **Buoyancy aid 50** – Swimmers only – not a life jacket.

(b)    **Life jacket 100** – Sheltered waters.

(c)    **Life jacket 150** – Offshore, foul weather clothing.

(d)    **Life jacket 275** – Offshore, extreme conditions and heavy protective clothing.

## Immersion suits

96    Immersion suits provide extended survival time in water by reducing the risk of cold shock and delaying the onset of hypothermia. They also make it easier to propel and get the wearer out of the water and make the wearer easier to find in the water to help aid recovery. Immersion suits come in two main types – constant wear and abandonment. Suits may be already insulated, or insulation may be provided by an inflatable liner. Uninsulated suits may be provided with a removable inner garment, or may require that specified clothing be worn to provide sufficient insulation to achieve expected survival times.

## Key points

97    Key points to note about life jackets/buoyancy aids and immersion suits are:

(a)    It is essential to consider all elements when selecting suitable equipment – body size; the weight of the person using it; the water and weather conditions; the likely rescue recovery time; the need for accessories (eg life jacket spray hood, light, body harness and line, locator beacon, whistle, immersion suit hood, gloves).

(b)    Ensure the immersion suit fits and no water can leak into it. Check that the suit chosen will not handicap the ability of the life jacket to keep the person's head above the water and to turn the person the right way up.

(c)    Note that anyone wearing inherently buoyant life jackets may be injured if they fall from a significant height. Note also that too much buoyancy may hinder escape in some circumstances, for example, from an upturned craft.

(d)    Inspect equipment at regular intervals. Check for wear and tear and damage. Check the inflation mechanism regularly as it can fail to operate if subject to rough handling or incorrect storage. Check the seals on the immersion suit are intact.

# Personal fall protection

## Types of systems

98    Personal fall-protection systems comprise an assembly of components for protection against falls from height at work, including at least a body-holding device connected to a reliable anchor. Such systems include **work-restraint** systems, **work-positioning** systems, **rope-access** systems, **rescue** systems and **fall-arrest** systems.

99　The equipment and components used may sometimes be the same within any of these systems – it is the manner in which they are used which determines the type of system:

(a) **Work-restraint** systems prevent the user from reaching zones where the risk of a fall exists. Such systems are sometimes incorrectly called 'fall restraint'.

(b) **Work-positioning** systems support the user in tension or suspension while a task is being undertaken in such a way that a fall is prevented or restricted. Such systems allow the user to have both hands free for working. However, work-positioning systems must always incorporate a back-up system (typically a fall-arrest system) designed to protect the user if the primary work-positioning system fails.

(c) **Rope-access** systems use two separately secured sub-systems, one as the means of support and the other as a safety back-up for (specifically) getting to and from the place of work. Such systems become work-positioning systems when the user is at the place of work. It is important to note that in such a system both ropes are static (ie stationary) while the user moves up and down the rope. If the rope supporting the user moves with the user (ie as in a bosun's chair arrangement) the system is a work-positioning system not a rope-access system.

(d) **Rescue** systems are personal protective systems by which a person can rescue themselves or others by pulling, lifting or lowering.

(e) **Fall-arrest** systems are personal protective systems where the fall is arrested to prevent the user colliding with the ground or structure. Such systems have energy absorbance capacity built into the system and are designed to limit the forces on the human body to no greater than 6 kN. Examples are energy absorbing lanyards, inertia reel devices (when used correctly, ie anchored vertically above the user) or lead climbing using dynamic rope.

## Key points

100 Key points to note about personal fall protection:

(a) Consider all elements when selecting suitable equipment – the maximum descent height and load; safe and secure anchorage points; the length, type and number of ropes and lanyards; the specification of ascender/descender devices; a system for recovery after a fall. Regulation 5 of the Lifting Operations and Lifting Equipment Regulations 1998 (LOLER) requires that equipment used for lifting or lowering people is safe.

(b) Inspect equipment at regular intervals. Regulation 9 of LOLER requires lifting equipment for lifting people to be examined every six months by a competent person if it is exposed to conditions causing deterioration which is liable to result in dangerous situations.

(c) Special care needs to be taken when inspecting components made from webbing and rope because of the deterioration that can take place in these materials. Guidance on this topic and the recommended inspection frequency can be found in INDG367 *Inspecting fall arrest equipment made from webbing or rope*.[5]

# Hearing protection

101 The PPE at Work Regulations do not apply to hearing protection except that it must be compatible with any other PPE provided. Full guidance on the selection, use, care and maintenance of hearing protection is given in L108 *Reducing noise at work: Guidance on the Noise at Work Regulations 1989.*\* Hearing protection should only be used where risks to hearing remain despite the implementation of other measures to control the noise, or while those other measures are being developed or put in place.

## Types of protection

102 There are two main types of hearing protection:

(a) **Earplugs** – These fit into or cover the ear canal, to form a seal. They sometimes have a cord or neckband to prevent them being lost. They can be permanent (indefinite use), reusable (use only a few times) or disposable (use once).

(b) **Earmuffs** – These are normally hard plastic cups, which fit over and surround the ears. They are sealed to the head by cushion seals (filled with plastic foam or a viscous liquid). The inner surfaces of the cups are covered with a sound-absorbing material, usually soft plastic foam. They can be headband or helmet mounted and some can have communication equipment built into them.

# Respiratory protective equipment

103 Full guidance on the selection, use and maintenance of respiratory protective equipment (RPE) is given in the HSE publication HSG53 *Respiratory protective equipment at work: A practical guide.*[4] If using RPE you need to refer to this document.

## Types of RPE

104 Respiratory protective equipment is generally of two types:

(a) Respirators that rely on filtering contaminants from workplace air. These include simple filtering facepieces and respirators and power-assisted respirators.

(b) Breathing apparatus, which gives an independent supply of breathable air, for example fresh-air hose, compressed airline and self-contained breathing apparatus. You will need to use breathing apparatus in a confined space or if there is a chance of an oxygen deficiency in the work area.

105 To make sure that the selected RPE has the potential to provide adequate protection for individual wearers, the Approved Codes of Practice supporting the Control of Substances Hazardous to Health Regulations 2002 (as amended), the Control of Lead at Work Regulations 2002, and the Control of Asbestos at Work Regulations 2002 require the fit testing of RPE which incorporates a tight-fitting facepiece. A tight facepiece is a full-face mask, a half-face mask, or a filtering facepiece.

---

\* New Control of Noise at Work Regulations will come into force in April 2006.

106   People who work with harmful dusts should not use nuisance dust masks to protect themselves from exposure. Nuisance dusk masks are not protective devices, are not classified as PPE and are not CE marked to the requirements of the PPE Directive. Nuisance dust masks, which are available from most DIY stores, consist of a thin metal plate that holds a piece of gauze over the nose and mouth or a lightweight filter that looks similar to a disposable dust respirator. Nuisance dust masks typically have only a single headstrap.

# References

1    *Consulting employees on health and safety: A guide to the law*
Leaflet INDG232 HSE Books 1996 (single copy free or priced packs of 15
ISBN 0 7176 1615 0)

2    *Five steps to risk assessment* Leaflet INDG163(rev1) HSE Books 1998 (single
copy free or priced packs of 10 ISBN 0 7176 1565 0)

3    *Reducing noise at work. Guidance on the Noise at Work Regulations 1989*
L108 HSE Books 1998 ISBN 0 7176 1511 1 (New edition due in October 2005.)

4    *Respiratory protective equipment at work: A practical guide* HSG53 (Third
edition) HSE Books 2005 ISBN 0 7176 2904 X

5    *Inspecting fall arrest equipment made from webbing or rope*
Leaflet INDG367 HSE Books 2002 (single copy free or priced packs of 10
ISBN 0 7176 2552 4)

## Further reading

This section includes the most useful Standards for selection, use and maintenance and also other relevant HSE publications. Many other Standards not listed here are relevant to specific risks or occupations. A list of current harmonised EU Standards can be found at: www. europa.eu.int/comm/enterprise/newapproach/ standardization/harmstds/reflist/ppe.html. British Standards are available from BSI Customer Services, 389 Chiswick High Road, London W4 4AL
Tel: 020 8996 9001 Fax: 020 8996 7001 e-mail: cservices@bsi-global.com
Website: www.bsi-global.com

### Head protection

*Construction (Head Protection) Regulations 1989. Guidance on Regulations* L102 (Second edition) HSE Books 1998 ISBN 0 7176 1478 6

### Eye and face protection

BS 7028: 1999 *Eye protection for industrial and other uses. Guidance on selection, use and maintenance*

### Hand and arm protection

*Cost and effectiveness of chemical protective gloves for the workplace: Guidance for employers and health and safety specialists* HSG206 HSE Books 2001 ISBN 0 7176 1828 5

*Selecting protective gloves for work with chemicals: Guidance for employers and health and safety specialists* Leaflet INDG330 HSE Books 2000 (single copy free or priced packs of 15 ISBN 0 7176 1827 7)

*Preventing dermatitis at work: Advice for employers and employees* Leaflet INDG233 HSE Books 1996 (single copy free or priced packs of 15 ISBN 0 7176 1246 5)

### Protective clothing (including the legs)

*Protect your feet: Advice for employees in the textile industry* Leaflet IACL84 HSE Books 1996 (single copy free)

BS 7184: 2001 *Selection, use and maintenance of chemical protective clothing. Guidance*

PD CEN/TR 14560: 2003 *Guidelines for selection, use, care and maintenance of protective clothing against heat and flame*

### High-visibility clothing

*Personal protective equipment (PPE): High visibility clothing for airport workers* Air Transport Information Sheet APIS1 HSE Books 1995 Internet only www.hse.gov.uk/pubns/APIS1.htm

### Foot protection

ISO/PFR TR 18690 *Guidelines for the selection, use and maintenance of protective occupational footwear* (currently in the later stages of development, with a projected publication date of October 2005)

### Drowning protection – buoyancy aids, life jackets and immersion suits

*Review of probable survival times for immersion in the North Sea* HSE Offshore Technology Report OTO 95 038. Available free at http://www.hse.gov.uk/research/otopdf/1995/oto95038.pdf

*Compatibility test protocol for lifejackets and immersion suits on offshore installations* HSE Offshore Technology Report 2002/021 HSE Books 2002 ISBN 0 7176 2347 5. Also available free at http://www.hse.gov.uk/research/otohtm/2002/oto02021.htm

### Personal fall protection

BS EN 363: 2002 *Personal protective equipment against falls from a height. Fall arrest systems*

### Hearing protection

BS EN 458: 2004 *Hearing protectors. Recommendations for selection, use, care and maintenance. Guidance document*

*Noise at work: Advice for employers* Leaflet INDG362 HSE Books 2002 (single copy free or priced packs of 10 ISBN 0 7176 2539 7)

*Protect your hearing or lose it!* Pocket card INDG363 HSE Books 2002 (single copy free or priced packs of 25 ISBN 0 7176 2540 0)

### Respiratory protective equipment

BS 4275: 1997 *Guide to implementing an effective respiratory protective device programme*

*Selection of suitable respiratory protective equipment for work with asbestos* Leaflet INDG288(rev1) HSE Books 2003 (single copy free or priced packs of 5 ISBN 0 7176 2220 7)

## Further information

HSE priced and free publications are available by mail order from HSE Books, PO Box 1999, Sudbury, Suffolk CO10 2WA Tel: 01787 881165  Fax: 01787 313995 Website: www.hsebooks.co.uk (HSE priced publications are also available from bookshops and free leaflets can be downloaded from HSE's website: www.hse.gov.uk.)

For information about health and safety ring HSE's Infoline Tel: 0845 345 0055 Fax: 0845 408 9566 Textphone: 0845 408 9577 e-mail: hseinformationservices@natbrit.com or write to HSE Information Services, Caerphilly Business Park, Caerphilly CF83 3GG.

The Stationery Office publications are available from The Stationery Office, PO Box 29, Norwich NR3 1GN Tel: 0870 600 5522 Fax: 0870 600 5533 e-mail: customer.services@tso.co.uk Website: www.tso.co.uk (They are also available from bookshops.)

Printed and published by the Health and Safety Executive    C150    08/05